Advance Praise for

The Perfume of Leaving

KB Ballentine's poetry embodies what James Wright called "the delicacy and strength of lace." Love and blues are her subjects, and she is faithful to them in lines that are firm yet fanciful, offering trellises with blooms in every season. Perhaps this is the "season of want," but in KB's hands the season is plentiful; the poems regale and nurture us, croon and soothe. *The Perfume of Leaving* is a gift that each song gives back after sorrow. From the elegant lyricism of "Blueshift" to the grudges "clutched like salt," our poet has the confidence and sureness of craft and spirit "to get it right / this time."
> — Marilyn Kallet, author of 16 books, including
> *The Love That Moves Me*, Black Widow Press

KB Ballentine's *The Perfume of Leaving* questions whether moments serve as arrival or threshold, blessing or sorrow. After all, we live in a context where "Eternity stains the air." So, too, memory–its possibilities, its promises, as well as its erasures, its regrets. Her poems offer a way to "refus[e] the news and its dirges,"–both national and personal, both present and past–despite recognizing that "the path to the future lies broken." Ballentine's poems stand clear, steadfast, aware that even though "the way ahead [is] unclear," we must "trust our hearts to that first step."
> — Jeff Hardin, author of *Small Revolutions* and
> *Restoring the Narrative*

In Celtic spirituality, thin places are where the physical and spiritual, the visible and invisible, merge. Ballentine's work is full of such places, where past and present meet as "ghosts swarm," and where the "moment of blessing, moment of sorrow" are one and the same. Ballentine studies "the names they left" for clues to how past loss produces present strength. In response to "What could I offer now?" she offers the answer of deeply observed details: "... surf spooling around our ankles / Fireflies, hope flaring in twilight." This book is itself "a pause between ridges that capture(s) the light" and the note of this book's perfume is all heart.

— Kimberly L. Becker, author of *Words Facing East* and *The Dividings*

In *The Perfume of Leaving*, KB Ballentine weaves alchemical word magic, with an astounding tenderness in vision and voice. Her poems are elegant jewels, with a powerful sense of place in the Appalachian Mountains. Her writing weaves sensual beauty, transparent emotions, and language that sings — poems running wild in the landscape of the heart. Her poems will call you to see the world in a different way.

— Diane Frank, author of *Blackberries in the Dream House*

the perfume
of leaving

Books by KB Ballentine:

What Comes of Waiting (2013), Blue Light Press
Fragments of Light (2009), Celtic Cat Publishing
Gathering Stones (2008), Celtic Cat Publishing

Anthologies containing her work:

River of Earth and Sky: Poems for the 21st Century (2015)
Southern Poetry Anthology, Volume VI: Tennessee (2013)
Southern Light: Twelve Contemporary Southern Poets (2011)
A Tapestry of Voices (2011)

the
perfume
of leaving

KB BALLENTINE

Blue Light Press   ❧   1st World Publishing

1ST WORLD
PUBLISHING

San Francisco | Fairfield | Delhi

Winner of the 2016 Blue Light Press Book Award

1st World Publishing
PO Box 2211
Fairfield, Iowa 52556

www.1stworldpublishing.com
Blue Light Press
1563 45th Avenue
San Francisco, California 94122
bluelightpress.com

⭐

Original Cover Painting
Michelle Young   *www.michelleyoung.com*

Layout
Jim Canestrari

ISBN: 9781421837635

Library of Congress Control Number: 2016950466

Acknowledgements

Many of these poems were conceived in the workshops of Diane Frank, Dr. Marilyn Kallet, and Bill Brown. Whether in San Francisco, Auvillar, or Sweetwater, these poet-mentors have guided and expanded my writing, and I am grateful for their wisdom, advice, and friendship.

To the Community of Writers at Squaw Valley, under the direction of Brett Hall Jones and also to Robert Hass, Brenda Hillman, Forrest Gander, Sharon Olds, and Evie Shockley, a special thank–you for your workshops that provided me a place to write, a place to explore my own work, and a place to grow as a poet, free to experiment with both form and subject matter; you teased open a cracked shell and allowed my work to fly.

For my family and friends who provide constant support, feed-back, and love, I cannot say enough. Without you, this book could not have happened. I am thankful, especially, to Helga Kidder, Karen Slikker, David Austin, Christine Connely, Graceful Beam, Michelle Young, Mary Kay Rummel, and the poets of the Chattanooga Writers' Guild. And to my husband, Jim, and my parents, Buddy and Susan, whose constant love give me confidence and strength, all my heart.

Grateful acknowledgement is made to the editors of the journals and anthologies in which these poems have appeared, sometimes in different forms:

2nd and Church	"Threshold" and "Perfume of Leaving"
Americana	"High Rises and Pigeon Parks" and "When Words Won't Come"

American Diversity Report	"Anniversaries," "Beyond the Silence," "Family Circus," and "Hialeah–Miami Springs, Then and Now"
Amore: Love Poems	"Seasonal Guide to Joy"
Avocet	"Blueshift"
Bindweed	"Refuge"
Blue Lyra	"Backscatter" and "For the Actors"
Blast Furnace	"A Litany of Hours"
Broad River Review	"Color of Longing"
Clementine	"After Midnight"
Front Range	"New Hope, Texas"
Gyroscope Review	"Island of Glass," "Memorizing Rain," and "Wanted: New Heart"
Haight–Ashbury Literary Jrnl	"Water Taxi"
Long Story Short	"Preserve"
Mountain Anthology	"Black Stone, White Stone: Reflection"
New Mirage	"In the District of Columbia"
One Trick Pony	"The Garonne," "In Praise," and "Fragments from Auvillar"
A Quiet Courage	"Courtship on Hold"
Red Paint Hill Review	"Ruins"
Shadowgraph	"After the Last Visitor Leaves" and "Harvesting Shadows"
Southern Light Anthology	"The Names They Left"
Still: The Journal	"Stone and Olive" and "Winter Reverie"
Sweatpants and Coffee	"Final Call"
A Tapestry of Voices	"Old School"
Tidal Basin Review	"Foreclosure"
Uproot	"Through Closed Doors"
Zingara Poet	"Winter Resignation"

"Ar scáthe chéilea mhaireann na daoine."

"People live in one another's shadows."

—Irish Proverb

Table of Contents

III.

IV.

I.

2   **the perfume of** leaving

Blueshift

Snowbroth shadows the fields,
      drifts deep in the woods,
puzzle pieces of mountain snow.

The solstice shivers its approach,
      desires the echo of summer seas
and roses blushing the garden.
      Eternity stains the air.
                Now
      white and blue ink lingering nights.

I can't remember the time before you,
      can't imagine harmony without the melody.
    Flakes gentle the sky then flurry down.
Tomorrow's night won't last as long.

The Shadow of Another

keeps you from me.
Swept with grain and gray
slanting Clomarty Firth,
the Black Isle hugs close the sea.
But you push away.

Gulls wail by the shore,
surf frothing rock,
evergreens leaning into the land.
You stand alone.
Horses thunder the field —
the sea calling.

Poison

Half–moon lounges in purple blush,
crushed acorns rotting under the struggle of fall.
Bees still worship the sweet gum tree
though a symphony of leaves swirl
through goldenrod — last bit of summer's
color shriveling in raw night.
Nights frosted with thoughts of you —
memories frozen in place though you've moved on.
If only I hadn't seen her reach for your hand, kiss you.
If only you hadn't let her.

Compressed

Daffodils torch the evening sky,
mist tumbling in with night.
Stars pulse beyond a harmony of clouds
and gnarled branches shake fists,
flaunting green though flurries
still sputter. The echo of your last words
etches the frosty air. I breathe them in,
feel them press my lungs from the inside out.
This is the moment of blessing,
moment of sorrow.

Wanted: New Heart

Dawn's breath pinks the sky,
a delicate yawn of gold and orange
as fog shifts the valley.
Yesterday's rain wrinkled the lake,
clouds veiling the mountain,
sailboats, kayaks shored
as last leaves fall. Sun slants lower,
spring as far away as those we forget.
These sharp days pierce my skin,
memories of flaming maples
haunting the honeycombs.

The Absence of You

I imagined your reflection in my smile —
that old photograph you snapped
when all I could do was look at you,
my love, my world.
Waves crested behind me,
crashed on rocky shore.

Oh, that my heart was like a bit of glass
polished clear by endless friction.
A broken shell, serrated edge waits
to pierce the careless wanderer
when low tide stretches long.

Oh, not to break, to bleed.
A drop of water, ounce of brine,
grain of sand, infinity of sting.

After the Last Visitor Leaves

Heat strafes the air, shock waves
of pressure against my skin.
Shadows crease corners of the yard.
Thin lines offer no respite
to black-eyed susans, blue hydrangea.

Behind the daily news,
your taciturn mask, our grief
still froths.
What will we do with all this food?

When you don't answer, I take the plates
to the kitchen — notice her pink sweater
hanging in the hall. Watch the clock
tick another second.

The Color of Longing

blushes outside my window —
a dogwood just bursting into bloom.
Dawn flutes us awake, and I reach
for your hand in the orange-gold light.
Your breath shallows, and you smile
in your sleep, pale shoulder begging
my lips. *I love you* — so simple
when robins tremble bare bushes
by the porch, and I snug into your warmth.
When your eyes drift open from dreams —
you whisper her name.

Certain Dark Things

I love you as certain dark things are to be loved,
in secret, between the shadow and the soul. —Pablo Neruda

Raven hovers, settles with a *cack,* a *caw.*
    Dreams shadow the room, whispers of   you
re–appear   in corners when I get out of bed —
    chunks   of darkness, they wait   for me to slip
under the covers. They'll edge   close,
    wings like the blackbird's rustling
    around my head,   feathering my cheeks
as I swallow   sleep, to dream again,
                of you.

Surrender

Between gasps of thunder, wind screams,
a smear of rain as lightning sears the sky bone–white.
Like weeds after summer rain,
you come to me on nights like this.
Thoughts of you piercing my mind like glass,
like ice chafing my skin raw by a winter's sea,
a bitter bite into garlic
that does nothing to hold you at bay.

You used to shape music for me
like water whispering over stone,
red wine gliding my throat,
like a spring evening slipping into summer dawn —
fear of night and chill vanished,
crumbling around my feet.

Through Closed Doors

Clouds stutter the blue.
Tipped in gold, an oak flirts with fall.
We circle, you and I —

too many times I've tripped
over the past, memories
I should have tossed.

And you —
you've waxed silence
into polished perfection.

Once, I knew you,
could translate nuances
slipping through your skin.

No more.
A shadow hovers
as we divide our lives —

the signed baseball, the blender —
mundane items we've clutched
since love stumbled away.

This morning my cup steams
and I step through empty rooms,
watch a butterfly drift over fences,

wings trembling.

Courtship, On Hold

Dawn breaks over the lake,
pink–capped clouds hanging heavy.

One last dragonfly glides the glossy surface,
ripples lingering behind.

Crickets and peepers wrap the air with static.
Summer closes quickly in the mountains,

shadows quilting the woods.
I think of the photos you send — the squalid camp,

sand thick and yellow crusting your clothes,
your face . . . . I want to stroke the smile

back into your eyes. Time licks the ribbon
on my tree, my breast, waiting for you.

Splintering

Stars spin the blackness. Clouds scoot
      the sky, woods flickering
            with sound, light.

Your note seared me,
      left a trail of scattered ash
            storms could not wash away.

Frogs trill and fireflies dazzle shadows,
      blink fire as fat drops slide through leaves,
            shatter against the dark night.

When Words Won't Come

after Bill Brown

Blinds tilt to shade the South Florida sun. A high hum fills the
air, and I spot his smile again, brief and rare, brown eyes
grinning, cold beer can wrapped — even now — in his hand.
Pipe smoke swirls the living room, tobacco leaves litter his olive
green chair . . . . Papa, What did you love? *I loved to meet
with the guys at the Legions Hall. Swap aches and pains for
memories of drills and routine.* What did you love? *Driving
you to the beach, stopping for cherry snow cones on the way
home, sticky kisses puffed in the rearview mirror.* What were
you thinking, always silent in your chair? *I was thinking of my
days at sea, how both waves and guns smashed against the
ship. Lonely metal bunks. Of my mother. How she reached
across the stove, how her sleeve caught fire. How I couldn't
put out her screams.* What will you miss? *I'll miss the taste of
strawberries pulled through my pipe, tapping leaves into its
firm brown bowl.* What will you miss, Papa? *The house, warm
with December days and all of you. Never telling my sons I
loved them.*

Clinging

At dawn's insistence, cardinals coax songs,
     swelling breasts beg and crave a bit of food —
          entrance to some Promised Land they sense at hand.

Bitter blue still stings —
     reminder that winter wraps my heart,
          icicles sliding through my blood.

A dime–sized fire pulses to an ancient
     store of wisdom. A wealth of verse,
          alchemy I cling to as wind shivers the firs.

Final Call

for Jodi

Surf trenches the pebbled shore,
saw–toothed rocks disappearing —
tide swallowing sand, foam sliding
back into the sea. Salt coats my throat,
and two crows argue with wind
that gusts my hair, calls you to mind.

City girl, gritty smile at school.
That first year you trudged to the cafeteria
bag hunching your shoulder,
hands plunged in pockets, chin rammed into scarf.
But you belly–laughed at our jokes,
teased as we trumpeted our loves,
recited "Sigh No More, Ladies" under the trees.

Too soon, you slouched in a small white room
shrouded in sheets, heart bleeping on a screen —
four walls your horizon.

A flock of gulls chuffs at the shoreline.
One steps out, catches the wind. Crow follows.

Island of Glass

Glastonbury, Somerset, England

The Tor towers over the hedgerows, the hazel,
cottage lights stippling the hill.
White bites my skin, ice shrouding the path.
Gray sweeps the horizon,
no distinguishing east from west,
up from down — meadow and peak topsy–turvy,
a monochrome model for the eye.

Frost floats like butterfly wings, pinks cheeks.
Yews stoop, layers of snow cracking,
sliding into piles that puff into chilled air.
Somewhere in the boxwoods a robin
whistles, reminds me I am not alone.
Not here where snow erases the horizon,
my promises. You.

Blurred

Night sheds its shimmer
as a frown of clouds moves in.
This morning I learn the rain,
sun sewn behind fog.
I steep tea, watch leaves bleed.
Sparrows temper their tune,
discreet cheeps,
distinct from yesterday's
chatter and song.
On bright days your memory
doesn't seduce me.
Today you hover
in the corners of shaded rooms.
I recoil from the radio —
melodies of promises unkept.
I used to love the rain.
Now it brings ghosts.

Suspended

October squanders oak,
infuses crimson through cascading sky.
Summer trimmed and sifted,
left on memory's sill of tides,
blossoming light.
Clouds cowl the hunter's moon.

These are the days of you I miss most —
campfire smoke, a quiver in the air,
apples hanging heavy,
                    begging to be picked.

Daylight Thins

Cedar waxwings flood the air
with melody, autumn bantered back
in red–traced maples,
oaks spreading gold.

Night swipes late rays
bridging branch to branch,
drizzle slows, blurs —
all shadows suspect in fog.

Ruins

Early chill and a spray of stars ignite
Orion's belt. Yesterday turkeys brooded
the backyard, flinched when I moved.
Today a fox trots across the field,
tail a copper flag in long rye grass,
flattened some places where the deer nest.
Refusing the news and its dirges
of war, disease, famine, death,
I scuff a leaf in the swelling darkness —
can't tell if it's bronze or still green,
tangled underbrush more bare,
robins hopping, poking for worms, gnats.
Ragweed dry and dusty,
lingering roses droop —
fading blush argues with crimson dogwoods,
blood moon climbing.

the perfume of leaving

II.

Stone and Olive

Your heart — hard and charred
like coal–mined mountains of Kentucky —
leaches dread, slithers like volcanic sludge
through my blood. Forget the sassafras
that pierces cracks, greens the gray —
graphite swollen and ceaseless
concealing the horizon of you.
Not enough mint or basil to seal the wounds,
to heal the scars of your past.
You clutch each grudge like salt,
smoke stinging the eyes,
blistering the nose with scorched smell of rubber.
Anger as smooth and heavy as slate,
not even a dove could fly away.

Winter Reverie

Geese V south, branches bleak
against noon blue. Snowfall last night
surprised, delighted us like deer tracks
under white–capped apples,
first flakes dusting the pines.
But blood scattered with feathers
and fur across batches of snow
remind us all is not at peace. Tonight,
under a waning moon, I will fly to you
before the season of want fully descends.

Injured

Shadowy room,
flashes of light.
Uniformed women
prod, wake me.
Rob my blood.

Erin, Dark Lady
of the ward, broods
by my bed at midnight.
Sister Mary Clare
bows close
in blurred morning.

Bleached sheets,
gown open,
tubes taped
to arms and legs.
Drips diffuse time.

I survived those days.
You didn't take
my hand.

Dusk

We walked toward the burning horizon,
yellow globe of harvest's moon swollen
behind us. You discovered a path unseen
before. *Want to try it?*

Of course. With you I'd try anything.
You smiled and squeezed my hand
then led the way. I watched your back,
moved as you did. Fell in love with you again.

The path ended by your house.
I didn't notice the stars, just the outlines of pines
against sky as night purpled around us.
The neighbor's dog barked
at a raccoon, our voices, a shadow.

Memorizing Rain

Emily had it right — *truth must dazzle gradually.*
Monarchs and mourning cloaks flicker the butterfly bush,
wings trembling in the dew.
Black walnuts drop through leaves,
a rustle and thud scattering the squirrels, my thoughts.

Stepping into drizzle, I remember waiting
for your phone call with her to end, for you
to welcome me as I sat outside in another rain.

You beckoned me in, slid your fingers down my cheek,
and your eyes revealed what our bodies refused.
Rain on roof, I learned your face through tears.
My body burns from that final time,
embarrassed — still wanting you.

Lichen–dappled bark looms beyond the porch
in the mist, bells echo the hour —
this last day of summer dissolving into night.

Hialeah–Miami Springs, Then and Now

for my parents

Saw palmettos sputter under autumn sun,
hibiscus burning bright in the landscaped parking lot.
Sand, salt cling to flip–flops, cola cans, skin,
scatter like a trail of breadcrumbs from car to store.

*

In 1965 checkered floors lacquered bright
at the East 2nd Avenue Publix,
blinding under brand new bulbs —
bouffants and beehives, minis and stilettos
waltzed in for the weekly chore.

He ruled the meat department,
white apron strings wrapped twice around his flesh,
knew a T–bone from a porterhouse,
how to slice ham fine for the office party.
     She, the green–smocked cashier, peering up
     from Archie and Betty comics to slide
     Jiffy Pop and Chiffon margarine past the register,
     summing up the total with a smile.

He and his gang swarmed the Everglades,
glass–faced and breathing air through tubes,
they outraced sharks, tangoed with eels —
     She and her friends surfed the waves,
     tumbled onto shore to wax the boards,
     tan under salty skies.

Punching in late, they met, hands catching on time cards.
He asked her name, added *One day I'll marry you.*
She laughed, cheeks flushed with sun.

*

The old store has altered its face now,
sambaed red and gold *sabor* with the original green,
plantains and ox tails stocked by the salsa,
Latino music dancing with the palms — a new twist.

Wistful

Azaleas blush late afternoon,
sun chases pouting clouds.
A wood thrush wrinkles the air
with song.

Dickinson, Frost, Kenyon —
those New England hearts who seared
words to paper, disturbed
the universe.

What can I offer —
seam of lavender
gem–colored books carving the wall
a scarred cheek
flashes of butternut among the pines
a hound snuffling night?

Darkness swamps the half risen moon.
Tonight I will sleep. Will not dream.

Leftovers

Black and white photo creased
along the edge snapped my father at six,
straw hat pushed back like the Duke.
Flaunting pewter pistol, sunlight bouncing
off barrel aimed at sky,
his stance dared anyone to tangle
with younger sister in gingham,
brother in diapers saddled into the Radio Flyer.

My grandparents died soon and sudden,
one following the other with barely a breath.
Stuck into a stripped album ready for trash,
my aunt found this picture and saved it
from collectors' hands.
This, the only thing my grandparents left —
never meant for me.

Crossing Ladoga

Ice films the flooded field. Snow lathers ditches, drapes spruce,
bows birches this late February. Sky gray. A barren scene at
first glance, but blurs of red nip around the feeder — cardinals
and a robin — flutter as I shift behind the window. How do
you tell the wild ones you're a friend? You prick my thoughts.
Every smile a proffered pearl. I knew you late on this road.
Your stories of Russia, the camps, barbed wire pierced my
easy life. How many beatings did it take to break you? What
could I offer now? I pointed out the sunrise, steam from coffee
cups swirling the early morning. The constancy of the tide, surf
spooling around our ankles. Fireflies, hope flaring in twilight.
Cushions still dimpled, the porch chair waits. A few white hairs
cling to wicker, but you will not be back. You are lost inside
yourself, mumbling your past to an empty room. No fences,
no bars. No windows to your soul. Walls of flesh and bone,
brown eyes faded and smudged with blue. No tracks on ice
where the lighthouse beckons, a skeleton flashing through
night. Outside, a stray tucks his tail, won't approach.

Reflection on Mother's Day

Other women were made to mother,
arms held open at the door
cookie dough ready to heat and serve.

I know how to feel the pull, the pain,
watch the water flow and drown,
how to bleach ruddy sheets bright.

Other women know how to sew,
know how to shop with thoughts
of others with a little something
                              to surprise.

I can sterilize the bedroom and the bath,
pack toys and stiff blankets into tiny boxes,
listen to the crooning radio.

There are no days to honor me,
no groups to join with tales to tell,
no hands reaching out, no voices calling.

Family Circus

Papa had the best chair in the house,
a tightrope overview he straddled daily.
Pipe smoke pervaded the big top —
his only comment on the circus below.

Eighth grade, World–War–educated,
his chapped hands popped beer tops,
cooked chocolate drops, hugged me.
When I scaled his silent aerie,

his broad lap held me, tobacco leaves
spiraling into the rings below.
Ringmaster and clowns teased me
to descend, a sideshow

of grimaces, waving arms.
Papa and I balanced
under a red and white striped sky,
staring at the darkness, the light.

Water Taxi

For two euros this three hour ride
                follows the course of the canal
   from Saint Mark to Santa Lucia.
                        Skimming water, eyes level with the wake,
with *vaporetti*, I snug my bag close.

                    Wash of water slaps the bow,
   other travelers face inward, ignore horizon of unyielding land —
           Scalzi, bridges, parks stringing the bank.
Head resting against a window, one man sleeps, unshaved, unwashed.
   I wonder if the motion of the boat rocks him to sleep,
               if sleep eludes his nights.

The rise and fall of his body calls to mind
                when I couldn't sleep as a baby,
     my parents fastened me into the carseat
and piloted the neighborhoods,
              humming motor and rolling motion
                      quieting my cries, swaying me to dreams.

             Is this man, face gaunt and drawn, dreaming now,
his hours on land so troubled
      this slow ride through the *Canalazzo* his only rest?
         No fear in this ancient city of hydras? Charybdis?
            No other monsters vile enough to keep him awake —
      no myth more merciless than real life?

Anniversaries

I thought of you yesterday.
You used to inhabit every breath.
Maybe I'll visit your father's grave —
the last place I saw you, your deceit
under a white November sky.
Maybe I'll send your daughter a card,
her birthday. Did you remember?
I called your mother,
told her how much she meant to me.
Her ready smile that skipped a generation.

These little anniversaries,
touchstones of our life together.
But you?
I haven't sent you anything.
You took so much,
shared it with someone else.
I've been split and spilled.
The gathering back took more than I had
and left me gasping.
I lie on the ground and consider the stars.
Let today be the last mention of you.

Making Myths

Islay, Scotland

Foam curls into the shore, massages stone, shell.
Kelp fans the sand, purple and green blades bunched,
pulse unplugged — forerunners of man
before he staggered out of the depths?

Gulls chuff overhead, shriek
at silver flashing through blue–green waves.
Why did my grandfather's grandfather walk away
from the tide, the time
trade blue on blue to watch the seasons pass
in bronze, umber, and gold?

No more water reflecting sky,
only cotton spooling across the fields.
Clay and coal, dizzy depths
and blackened fingers,
creases that never came clean.

Here, the horizon shimmers just past my grasp,
wishful moonrise wrinkling midnight's surface,
regret crawling from the deep.

Beyond the Silence

Whispers from the walls conquer the silence of the street. Memories surge through me — you mowing the lawn, planting roses; her pink elephant, fingers scrunched in bow-shaped lips. Whispers from the walls remind me I'm alone, lost now in this too big house. I stroke the chintz in our room. Walk past the yellow and lamb nursery where we planned at least a quartet of new residents. Moving room to room, I ignore pictures of your face, her face: our family shattered. This path to the past brings your touch, her voice. But the path to the future lies broken, ruined without you. The silent street isn't loud enough to swamp whispers from the walls. I long to lean into your arms, feel you breathe against my hair — safe in your circle. I ache to comb her curls into pigtails that refuse to hang straight, her freckled grin and milk moustache. But this growing silence floats through the street, still can't drown whispers from these walls.

The Names They Left

Blue Ridge Mountains

Passing houses brown with mildew, damp
on a raw March day, the Spitfire chugs
the road, wind snatches my hair. Shadows drop

long and low across the buildings, the bridge.
A town of hope huddled in a cleft between ridges,
Sunbright chased by rivers around the mountain.

Who were the men and women who slashed,
stamped their way through underbrush
to get here — leading horses, hauling furniture

from another life, another world? One more genteel,
more polished; less dangerous, less alive. Why?
Why slop through mud and muck, drag children

through wild brambles, plucking blackberries
in July, hunting grouse in December?
Once here were they trapped —

only peaks ahead and foothills, disappointments
behind? Was this a refusal to fail one last time?
Look at the names they left. Bitter Creek.

Was it the water's taste? Did too many lose
wives and children to disease, crops to flooding?
Rock Creek bounding one side, Black Wolf the other.

Sunbright. A pause between ridges that captured
the light, held it for a moment. Ghosts swarm.

III.

Preserve

Rough–tongued raspberry skirts
the artless field, filters sun, rain,
the willful moon. Just yesterday
our sons embraced pails full of red
to greet you at noon, bloody juice
smearing shirts, staining hands.
Your nod, lingered phone call revealed all.

Today I listen to you limping
toward another excuse. Steam
spools from boiled jars flickering
in the sun. Kitchen window frames
the stale yard, the broken swing.
I've fooled myself, pretending
you'll fix it, this. Clouds whisk
blue, your voice dissolves to static.

Signs

In the Gulf sludge drifts on the tide,
across The Pond Germany rescues Greece,
and China's products idle in the motherland.
Am I safe in my own house — will the walls
that enfold me tonight be mine tomorrow?

Outside, robins nip grass under the chestnut.
Blue trembles through clusters of green.
The forsythia you planted last year
glows in gathering dusk, awaits your return.
Leaf and sky shrivel, merge into shadow.

In darkness I return to the house where the tv
natters, switch it off, silence swelling.

Learning Winter

Firethorn berries flare the snow,
       rival the cardinal's crest.
     January, and sleet will come soon,
          thick and quick.
            Each of these days is a lesson in you —
raw, stinging.

Threshold

Stars glitter the heavens tonight,
Leo's heart paling with Virgo's rise,
and I think of you — this time without regret.

I've shut the drawers —
all we did with all we wanted.
Shadows swallow what's left

of its light, sweet lavender.
Each star a wish I made —
to have, hold, keep you.

The stars scatter in patterns
of light that spin the seasons,
suddenly dazzling, dimming.

I search the sky. Centaurus gallops the horizon.

Autumn Nostalgia

Uncertainty quivers my insides —
last rays of October light echoing the leaves.
Years past found us tented under oak and sycamore,
trails threaded the woods, hawks spiraling overhead.
Your taciturn face holds my thoughts —
memories shaped like water, fluid and as changing.
You harbor regrets, I know.

The air smokes with camp fire, earthy loam.
A screech owl's descant punctuates
crickets and frogs. Red plum ripens
next to honey mushrooms, swirl of leaves tapping
the canopy above our heads. Oh, if I had it to do again,
the answer is *yes.*
Yes.

In Praise

Auvillar, you remind me of home —
palm trees and fig, terra-cotta tiles
    sun melting through the showers

Oh, Auvillar, you are *frais* —
Ronsard roses larger than my fist
    crumbling church in the sleepy hills,
                       the hills

You are contradiction —
river of death, of life, curls through you
   a boat, a bridge
brick walls and graffiti halo orange and cherry trees
pilgrims weary your cobbled streets
                and villagers call their dogs home

The drowsy moon dissolves in rain and day
children hopscotch the schoolyard
a ball rolls down the road,
              nestles into iris and calla lilies

Blue sky and cottonwood shade await —
faerie flakes blowing my wishes —
   here, not here —

And you, Auvillar, wait for me
           to see all of you —
old men dozing on benches
    women tossing sorrow into the Garonne

Foreclosure

Slapping air, a sparrow nulls the silence.
Thrushes of song gouge the pre–dawn
glow, goad me from hard–won sleep.

I segue from dream to thought, not ready
for this day. My Chevy crouches in the drive,
packed. I roll over, glimpse mangled shadows of boxes.

Watch sunrise here one last time.

New Hope, Texas

1934

Bristles of weed mangle
the once–swept yard. Wind
spits dirt into every crevice,
goads housewives, farmers
as tomatoes and peas segue
into shriveled pulp.

Patience dissipates, nulls
expressions of care into care–worn.
Even the cows are weary.
John Deere Model D rusts
in the sun, metal skeleton
gouging an indifferent sky.

Old School

He mimics his father, slouching
with thumbs hooked through jeans.
The girl will become her mother,
another unmapped journey.
For every man who reaps his acres,
there is a woman folded, creased
within walls, her route shelved.
Even counting the hens, visitors are few.

She fuels the stove, fries eggs and bacon,
sends husband and older sons
into the pre—dawn to taste the wind or choke
in its dust. She propels the younger children
across fields, steers their sleepy bodies
to discover a world she no longer misses.

Sun unchains behind the ridge, she boils
water and strips beds, tosses worn sheets
into a kettle to boil away stains. Eyes
searching the hillside, she picks beans
and tomatoes, lays some aside for canning
— bright greens and reds caught, ready
to suspend in row after row of sealed glass.

Her oldest daughter comes over the knoll
with the neighbor boy holding her arm,
one thumb hooked into his jeans.

In the District of Columbia

Hummingbird slips through rain,
    green shimmers the gray

Fog thickens, presses windows
    as hydrangeas purple the unraveling yard

Branches rib the sky,
    scratch the fading moon

Stars stitch the Potomac's wake,
    slap midnight's shore

Trains rumble tunnels, clatter tracks,
    stall by walls of names

Halls empty, doors locked
    a man slides down a marble column

his body grafted into the shadow

The Perfume of Leaving

Mid–March and fireflies already star the dark.
Jasmine and honeysuckle base notes linger in heavy air,
storms moving in after midnight the weatherman said.

Winter waned early, grass still green
as flakes whispered, melted into blue skies.
Spring's top notes evaporated in an early heat wave,
crocuses and daffodils bright then brown.

The heart of summer has yet to arrive
and already earth's fragrance burns —
the echo of dry days knocking tomorrow's door.

Winter Resignation

A shower of snow, ice dust drifting.
Hands so cold they burn, and hot pink memories
of bougainvillea, musk rose burst
into my mind. You, sitting in a grass field, head turned
away from me, the first clue.

Wind picks up, and I tug your old sled
up the track–scabbed hill, lift our son's small body
onto the graying wood. Watch him laugh and tip
into a pool of space before he, too, speeds away.

The Groundhog Disturbed His Shadow

March wind blisters the tangle of daffodils,
shears golden trumpets into withered pouches.
Sheets snap on the line, whorl of white
against gray skies, redbuds purpling
the woods beyond. Flurries loop branches
just greening — surprising spring,
twisting her promises, turning us into unbelievers.

Night Watch

In the beginning your words
gentled around me like a silk cape
then spread colder.
In our young bed your touch swirled my senses,
your caress on my face,
my body igniting.
Then empty, twisted sheets.

Last night clouds wrapped the new moon,
and flakes fell like tiny stars,
creating constellations around bare hydrangea limbs,
the feathered pines.
By midnight, all was dark again,
yard swallowed in shadow, snow sighing
goodbye.

Remnants of the February sky —
cold, expanding black.
Sirius shimmers briefly. A moment of hope,
even if I don't believe.

Litany of Hours

Long after my grandmother died
I learned her language of growing things.
Lantana, aralia thrived under her touch.
She never sang, but I heard her urging
the hibiscus, the canna lilies,
Birds of Paradise so high
they thrashed the house during storms.

She never cried, never offered a shoulder
when I burbled into tears,
only glanced my way with a frown,
resumed swirling sauce, grating mozzarella.
Late afternoons, sunlight draped the lanai
before she tucked her curls into a latex cap,
settled into the pool when we wearied
of splashing around.

Weekdays, Grandma's navy suit still crisp
when she returned those long Florida evenings
from a litany of hours transcribing,
she and daylight wandered among bursts
of flower pots topped with water,
shears ready to clip the strays.

My thumb doesn't have her gift for green.
Longings don't surge
through my fingers to touch seedlings
so they sprout, nurtured by a lifetime
of yearning that never spoke a word.

Harvesting Shadows

How do I say you were
the love of my life
without sounding cheesy, clichéd?

Picking cherries in Auvillar I think of you —
strawberries and late spring picnic with snow.
We huddled in the park,

devoured each other
under the flurries. Fire that sparks
graying twilight.

Deep green brushes heavy on my face.
All these leaves make it so damn difficult.
Like you.

Hard to get,
harder to keep,
and I didn't succeed.

The night I waited in the bar
for you — the first time
I said *I love you* —

you looked out the window,
turned your back. Twenty years later your smile
still charms, you don't see me.

You watched for failure,
for betrayal — and that's what you got,
even from this loyal lapdog.

The fruit under this azure sky is sweet
and bright. The ladder unsteadies my stance.
I drop some of my treasure, watch it bruise.

The Gift

I staggered under your rage, your mute panic
that filled each room.
Autumn crackled, you battled weather to strip the fields.
As long as I kept pace you endured my presence.
Then gray days of winter confirmed my faults,
there for the cursing.
Spring was remorseless, its gifts
of green and yellow stirring memories —
best friend piloting cone first into the dirt,
sister spinning over a car hood while you watched.
Spring with clouds that stain and puff through blue,
spring when you let me go.

Invocation

You left the last day in April, a blizzard
of dogwood petals icing the trees.
Dawn broke through branches flaked green,
drifts of daffodils thawing ferns.

May the cold moon disappear,
leave starshine and black satin.
Let hope melt any wayward snows.

May your summer linger long
after I'm gone.

Refuge

She handed me a stone, a leaf, a mustard seed.
I kept them safe, pillowed on pink satin,
read to them every day, hummed
my grandfather's red harmonica sometimes.
The house tilted, hollowed when she left,
spilling grief in her absence.

Mismatched hearts choked in our house
where incendiary streaks of anger blurred
each dinner, each new dawn.
The seed, the leaf dried then cracked,
bits of dust gathering and blowing away.

Under hushed violets and hesitant snows
the stone still pulses, traces of pink clinging.
A reminder of shadowed nights,
a blanket, her hands tucking me in.

Back Home

The rain tree my parents planted when I was ten
still splashes gold, blossoms dripping
from branches beside the broken sidewalk.
I slow the car, gape at slumping shutters,
glass door unhitched, waiting
for wind or hard knock to settle its next move.
Gone, the bushes shading Patch's grave, sheared
by power trimmers, someone lengthening the lawn.
Walnut and red maple vanished,
a little run–down, the house remains
much the way I remember —
kids running in and out,
my mother's face in the kitchen window,
my father about to turn in the drive.

On a Cloudy Day

Dawn struggles to splinter clouds
      that spun in with night.
  Conversations splash
    through my mind as I grate gears
down the mountain road.
Fog presses against the car,
bits of rain spit the windshield.
      Absurd weather
for such things as passion.
Today calls for kisses
    tendered down the neck,
whispering warmth from a lover's hand.
      And yours has let me go.

IV.

the perfume of leaving

The Way to Kilfenora

Rain silvers the road, spools
roof, window, hood —
showery outburst eases,
mist feathers the fields,
vacant light fading behind the ridge.

I start the car, hair un–pillowing
against the head rest. Road signs
crammed at crossroads
  — or none at all —
tattered atlas my bible
on this forgotten road,
I begin again.
Try to get it right
this time.

From Limerick to Cork

Soft day. Fogged sky. Mizzling. Headed south on the N20,
every mile a skein of ruins, lives brushed by. At Ballybeg Friary
thatch consumes stone, man's creation crumbling into fists of
rubble. Cows weave through the open framework, droppings
stitched where monks once laced vellum with words and knots,
threaded chants through the cloister. More drizzle from gray
wool skies. Cars and lorries *shush* the road. Down to the Island
Tomb, folded for centuries into a field, plundered then sutured
by scholars. I step whiddershins to snap photos — foxglove
purples the entrance shrouded with midriff grass, memories
of druids binding their dead. The sky collapses. I rush to the
Dorgan's barn, hay and warped wood wrapping familiar
scents around me, wet needles clatter on the tin.

Brú na Bóinne

[W]hisper to us of hope and new beginnings at the festival of
Imbolc. —Carole Carlton

The Boyne curves, whispers like swirling silk
through field, over stone — tossed checkerboard
of gold and green spread under mizzling sky.

Imbolc tints hazel and ash, a chill still coating
the stone of the seven suns. Pied wagtails,
skylarks whistle and stir the hedgerows.

Twilight, and the womb of the moon waits.
Like heartsease curled, eager for a vein
of light to flush, unfurl her bloom.

Backscatter

Stroma, Scotland

You remember only *Coinean*, the quilted bunny
stuffed with straw Mam replenished each summer,
ears droopy and soft, nose all but worn off.

Farmhouse sighs, wind hammering each broken board,
timber chopped and brought across the water
in *bátannach* too small for furniture.

Gannets and cormorants marble the rocks
with guano, scream as they skim eel grass
shifting in surf, fish scattering.

Light threads the splintered door. Outside,
buttercups beckon, waves crash against rock,
splash high — above you, the house.

Thistle sprouts in the collapsing kitchen.
          And the spoon. It glints against soil,
rusts with briny air. You pick it up,

memory shining on the possibility of this:
oatmeal, warm and gleaming with honey,
a small fire, peat smoke earthy and salted,

small hands knitting a sock — laughter fading
from the room as sharp gusts shriek
around a corner of crumbling wall . . . .

Fire evaporates with the sting of spray.
You are left to linger with relics of home
vanishing each day, reclaimed by wind and tide.

Kissing in Duntulm Castle

Isle of Skye, Scotland

Wind buffets the bay, the gulls, a finger of land
that dares the Minch's fury.
Chickweed and sea asters blossom,
sheep munching at rocky edge.
Fishermen embroider hooks, fill creels with mackerel,
electric blue netting shocking our eyes from shore.

We've frittered the day — picnic, rooting through ruins.
We scrabbled through slender thistle, scattered stones,
kissed behind grassy knolls sheltered from spray.
Collapsing windows only witness to the western isles,
staircase crumbling to gray nuggets.

We wonder if Lady MacLeod watched
the setting sun from here.
Held hands with someone who treasured her
as reddening sky blazed into sea.

Drought

Summer scabs blue, burns
even shadows. What happened
to the symphony of spring? Buds tumbling
from green, wood thrushes seducing dawn?
Waking to your chest roughing my cheek,
heart bumping cadence with mine
                              — days of promise.

August hisses across the yard, crows
emerging with twilight's dim breeze,
coolness lingers in the bed. Every morning
surprises my arm, my face to an empty pillow,
the impression of your body fading.
                              Today, no rain.

Lament

River slices the gorge, rock stacked
like beehives on both sides of the bank.
Icy water spills from mountain top,
and we pause to seek the sun, pale and high,
between branches scraping winter blue.

Day lengthens but we don't speak,
hike instead through crisp leaves
and withered apples, snow capping
everything woolly white.

You empty your pack by pine-bristled outcrop,
boots steady on the edge of stone.
Never glancing at me, you unseal and tilt
the jar. Sharp wind tears at our backs,
steals ash and bone, flings it into the void.

The Iceman Departs

Spring comes late to the mountains,
arroyos, mesas still rimed with white.
Daylight urges buds to uncurl, spear the dirt.
Pines brush the sky, dogwoods trailing close.
White clouds blow April into May.

House shuddering from the neighbor's bass,
I curl into solitude. News from the world intrudes
on tv: house fire, missing teen, hiker lost.
There's enough trouble here without searching
for more. With my look, you change the channel.

Though ice still streaks riverbanks, badgers
yawn, stir. Starling's shadow skims
the blue as jay wings incise north wind.
A woodpecker taps his territory.
A bee bumbles, drifts from bush to bush.

A Story Begins

Rain pounds pear trees, petals dropping
like snow, sudsing puddles with blossoms.
Ditches fill, sluice dirt, gravel across the road.
Windows smudge, and day slides darkly
around the oaks.

The pit in my heart dissolves,
step lighter as I clean house, wait for your call.
Headlights in the drive surprise. You splash
to the house where I open wide the door.

At Chickamauga Battlefield

Rain kisses rocks, a soft sucking
sound this late March morning.

Pink and white magnolia buds cloud
the distance, horizon a line of ash.

Throats of daffodils curve
submission to wind, yellows

and greens please the eye. Leaves
from last September wrap leather–like

around snowdrops, spiked shoots
of wild columbine lance the earth,

soon to be a field of red.

Stalled

I'm not ready for this yet.
Your words punch my mind.
Clouds scatter light, repent.

I sag into the seat, stomach clenched,
breath tight. Your touch last night
led to different thoughts. Future thoughts.

Gray converges, collapses over bits of gold. Rain.
My wrist exposed between us, your fingers stroke
pale skin where my pulse drops a beat.

Other People's Art

Clay stiffens in its mold, saffron and azure
dulling as they dry. Chipped marble embellishes
the borders. Charcoal and oils clutter
the table. Blank canvases stacked, wet ones
lining the room, I scrub pigment scabbing
the formica, bunch brushes into a cup.

Rain stripes the north windows. Like ballast,
clouds anchor the darkening sky. Glass
and light stamp my reflection on fading green,
burgeoning ochre outside. Another square,
another mold — boundaries.

High-Rises and Pigeon Parks

after Douglas Goetsch

You city poets deem you've got it, speeding
the freeway between Chicago and Boston
so it flashes past picket fences, blind
eyes behind newspaper clichés, call it *vibrant*
— and now you pen a poem from grit, push past
sirens crying through high-rises, pigeon parks.

But we are made of sunsets we can hold
long after the light has left, where darkness
shrugs close and kind around our shoulders.
Birch and poplar bend to whisper their secrets,
daisies, four o'clocks gild summertime,
fireflies the only flickering neon.
Solitude stolen by a cardinal in frost,
warming the window.

Muted

Cheshire cat moon grins, peeks
from smoky clouds — stars crisping
a blanket of black. Silence shrouds
this snowy night, breathes
a frosty fog across the pines.

What happened to lavender,
to meadowsweet? To grass sheathed
with dew? The sea of apple blossoms
seducing bees to their sacred center?
Hummingbirds tonguing honeysuckle
as it spills over the fence line?

No — it's ice tonight. White swelling
the tree–line, acres of promise breathing below.

Butterfly Effect

Feverish rain pocks the woods,
sculpts leaves into shivering veils.

Drops grip cobwebs, shudder
with news from Paris, Maiduguri.

Fear scents our skin,
fig musk purpling the shadows.

And the roots of oaks explore
sudden silence, puddles pooling —

our breath vapor. Flared, gone.

For the Actors

after Edward Hirsch

Tonight I want to tell you I believed
in your world so much that I went
home unburdened, purging myself of tears

that had built up for weeks, months, years.
Worry's worn path eased after rehearsals and bows
had taken their toll, discarded costumes a relief.

I love the way actors offer their entire being
to the madness or the song–joy,
the essence of their souls to the character,

letting its light shine or its evil corrupt
their faces, bodies, like demi–gods creating
a new universe, continents of power, hate, love.

And always they become themselves again.
Or nearly so. Altered by another's silky words, I want
to say: *Metamorphosis makes my heart sing.*

Our hearts like an empty stage, spotlights
chasing shadows from bare corners.
Music of arias, operas ghosting the air,

vibrating with the memory of applause.
Skin of so many others auditioning to be heard,
the art of silence throbs, aches our veins.

We must trust our hearts to that first step.
Floorboard squeaking, hum of voices,
of pulsing stardust, waiting for the cue to begin.

Performance seizing us by the throat,
the soul, until the curtains close, lights fading
on roses tossed and trembling.

The Garonne

Auvillar, France

When I let the river answer
   instead of the tolling bell
      that measures each breath of my day —

      instead of deep basses, chattering
   grunts and squeals of frogs
that echo my busy thoughts —

When I let the river answer
   instead of the wind fussing grasses,
      sun targeting some things, leaving others in shadow —

      When the cottonwoods sigh their blooms —
      When beaver dams dry high on the banks —
When poplars scribble green across the sky —

ripples soften time's illusions,
   wavelets lapping *legato, largo*
      fluid and static, a center, balance restored

Black Stone, White Stone: Reflection

after César Vallejo

I will die on a Tuesday morning, a storm spinning past
on a day I've already witnessed,
I will die in Connemara, or on my porch,
perhaps, on a day like today in April.

It will be April because in April, near the mountains,
dogwoods whiten thick–branched woods, and red clover sways
into golden fields of rapeweed, redbuds flushing the sky.
Breeze chills and warms, rushes fists of leaves.

She has just died, they will say as cardinals and finches chatter,
rain hanging heavy in the east, but sun trembling through clouds.
Puddles shiver with petals and maple seed wings.

And the morning will shift, swell brighter,
rays veining the pen between my fingers, a book open
at my side, pages thick with honey.

Fragments from Auvillar

The Garonne's ancient voice chimes
     and slips past Chapelle Ste Catherine.
          Faerie fuzz drifts from cottonwood trees
past empty dock rings.
     One hundred gates hide houses
          where women sip despair and licorice,
score the remains of their hearts onto paper —
          ready to toss sorrow into the tide.
Dreams flounder on concrete docks,
     gasp for air, choke on the perfume
          of hidden dung beetles.
Je suis désolée, the river sings,
     light and shadow waffling its surface —
          paper and hope kicking in the current.

After Midnight

Fog smears the valley,
ribbons of cherry blossoms
pinking dark woods.
Your memory tempts me,
lures me into the mist
where a grouse cackles,
something scampers in shadows.
Tiger lilies line the road, lead me
in bursts of orange this dull day.
Rivaling these mock suns,
a robin sings, doesn't nitpick
dawn's delay —
the way ahead unclear.

Seasonal Guide to Joy

The ribbon of your love follows me through the days,
    a tug that nudges a smile though winter's icy
        fingers scrape my scalp.
  When I weep under willows thick and green
fireflies sparkle the darkness,
    magnolias blushing sweet, heavy air.
      Fading days thrust bare and bleak,
  crackling ash leaves rage —
    whispers feathering my cheek.
When hope and growing seeds burst forth
  our love stretches far, holds me fast —
    clouds tumbling and tumbling the blue.

Glossary/Notes:

"Water Taxi" (p38)　　*vaporetti*: water buses
　　　　　　　　　　Scalzi: Church of St. Mary of
　　　　　　　　　　Nazareth (Chiesa di Santa Maria di
　　　　　　　　　　Nazareth)
　　　　　　　　　　Canalazzo: Grand Canal

"In Praise" (p50)　　*frais*: fresh, cool

"Backscatter" (p72)　　Stroma is an abandoned island off
　　　　　　　　　　the northeast coast of Scotland. The
　　　　　　　　　　last residents left their island home
　　　　　　　　　　in 1962. *The houses ... have rotted*
　　　　　　　　　　at different rates. Inside some ...
　　　　　　　　　　everyday objects still remain where
　　　　　　　　　　they were left decades ago.
　　　　　　　　　　　—Bella Bathurst

　　　　　　　　　　coinean: rabbit
　　　　　　　　　　bátannach: boats

"Fragments" (p87)　　*Je suis désolée*: I am sorry

About the Author

KB Ballentine received her MFA in Poetry from Lesley University, Cambridge, MA. She has participated in writing academies in both America and Britain and holds graduate and undergraduate degrees in English.

She teaches high school theatre, creative writing, and English and adjuncts for two local colleges. She has also conducted writing workshops throughout the United States.

Published in numerous literary journals, KB also received the Dorothy Sargent Rosenberg Memorial Fund Award in 2006 and 2007.

Learn more about KB Ballentine at www.kbballentine.com.

www.ingramcontent.com/pod-product-compliance
Lightning Source LLC
Chambersburg PA
CBHW032019090426
42741CB00006B/658